Power Learning in the Classroom

Jamieson A. McKenzie

CORWIN PRESS, INC.
A Sage Publications Company
Newbury Park, California

For information address:

Corwin Press, Inc.
A Sage Publications Company
2455 Teller Road
Newbury Park, California 91320

SAGE Publications Ltd.
6 Bonhill Street
London EC2A 4PU
United Kingdom

SAGE Publications India Pvt. Ltd.
M-32 Market
Greater Kailash I
New Delhi 110 048 India

Printed in the United States of America

Library of Congress Cataloging-in-Publication Data

McKenzie, Jamieson A. (Jamieson Angus), 1954-
    Power learning in the classroom / Jamieson A. McKenzie.
        p.   cm.
    Includes bibliographical references.
    ISBN 0–8039–6056–5
    1. Education—United States—Data processing. 2. Educational techology—United States. 3. Classroom management—United States.
I. Title.
LB1028.43.M38   1993
370'.973'0285—dc20   93–10946

93 94 95 96   10 9 8 7 6 5 4 3 2 1

Corwin Press Production Editor: Marie Louise Penchoen

Contents

Foreword

In *Power Learning in the Classroom,* Jamie McKenzie presents the array of new instructional technologies as providing the basis for an educational Renaissance, aimed at creating a generation of citizens prepared for the Information Age. He focuses on the need for a timely transition from a smokestack curriculum to one that produces *infotectives*—skilled thinkers, researchers, and inventors.

Chapters devoted to the major traditional academic content areas give specific examples of how the new technology can be used to enhance learning and insight. Social studies is described as evolving into a data-gathering and exploratory learning experience, with students acquiring expertise in information management, visual literacy, and reasoning. Similar experiences and outcomes are illustrated for instruction in math and science, which is also enhanced by electronic visual and manipulation/simulation learning opportunities. These multisensory capabilities also profoundly change the teaching and learning of English and the arts, enabling the development of the creative problem-solving skills needed in all types of work today—and in all areas of life.

Throughout the text, snapshots—scenarios of potential real-life student instructional and learning situations—provide glimpses

of the practical applications of the new technologies to education.
Jamie McKenzie gives us a look over the horizon at the powerful
learning that will be available in the classrooms of this decade—
and the new century.

JERRY J. HERMAN
JANICE L. HERMAN
Series Co-Editors

About the Author

J amieson A. McKenzie is President of Network 609, an educational consulting firm in Nantucket, MA. Before becoming a full-time writer and consultant, he served in many administrative and teaching positions, including superintendent; assistant superintendent; elementary principal; assistant principal of a middle school; departmental supervisor; teacher of English and social studies; adjunct professor at Douglas College, Rutgers; and teacher of 4-year-olds in Sunday school. He received his BA from Yale, his MA from Columbia Teachers College, and his EdD from Rutgers.

An early pioneer in the use of educational technologies, he has been successful in winning major grants from Apple Computer, Commodore, and other sources, grants that were used to produce state-of-the-art multimedia labs in his last two districts. He has established educational foundations in two school districts and has successfully developed business-education partnerships.

McKenzie has published many articles and presented at many national conventions on such topics as new technologies, educational futures, site-based decision making, teaching for thinking, and team building. He is the author of two books—*Making Change in Education: Preparing Your Schools for the Future* and *Site-Based Management: A Practical Guide for Practitioners*—and he is seeking a publisher for his first novel, *Coal Creek Rebellion*.

Introduction

When new technologies arrive on the scene, old mind-sets and patterns of behavior—the smokestack paradigms that have outlived the industrial economy they once served—often are limiting factors in fulfilling the new potential. *Power Learning in the Classroom* is dedicated to the belief that learning can be both more engaging and more productive with the computers, videodisc players, and other new tools of the Information Age. But school leaders must be prepared to shed those outmoded or irrelevant mind-sets; they must be ready to take a fresh look at the ways schools are organized for instruction and learning.

New educational technologies promise to open the doors and windows of American classrooms so that the world becomes the classroom and students become powerful thinkers—what Alvin Toffler would call "brainworkers." Properly utilized, new technologies can provide the basis for an educational Renaissance that will develop a generation of imaginative problem solvers well-equipped to handle a turbulent age of information.

This book presents technology applications with enormous capacities to empower students as thinkers, researchers, and inventors. These applications call for a shift in the roles of both teachers and students, but the shift is a necessary step for this society and economy—what Joel Barker would call a "paradigm shift."

The reader will find here a vivid road map to guide local school program development. Like any good road map, it offers a variety of routes, but much like a AAA *TripTik*, this book also warns the reader of obstacles and hazards that might interfere with implementation.

As of this writing, there is still evidence that technology has failed to penetrate the everyday life of most American students. Although there are hundreds of enterprising schools and teachers exploring the potential of new technologies, smokestack paradigms persist in most schools and most classrooms. New equipment often sits idly by or becomes the personal property of a handful of enthusiastic pioneers.

Power Learning maintains that the use of new technologies to make meaning is basic to citizenship and employment in the Information Age. Schools are responsible for implementing these technologies so that they permeate learning across all disciplines and classrooms. Within these pages, the reader is taken up into the "crow's nest" to peer over the horizon at the magnificent educational possibilities that lie just ahead. Once glimpsed, these possibilities may guide future navigation and program development so that decisions maximize benefits and avoid the shoals of trendy use of resources.

The Student as Thinker, Researcher, and Inventor

Imagine this scenario for the concept of *power learning*: New technologies open new educational windows, changing where and how students learn. Schools become information hubs, orchestrating the flow of data across complex networks, linking students and educators across towns and nations. The student's role is changed to a combination of thinker, researcher, and inventor; the teacher's role becomes a combination of guide, coach, and mentor.

An age of information requires changed conceptions of schooling and the creation of Toffler's "brainworkers," a generation of young people capable of thinking on their feet, finding answers to puzzling questions, and developing imaginative solutions to challenging problems (Toffler, 1990). In order to maintain the health and wealth of this society in the global Information Age, roles of students will shift from consumption of information and insight to production of insight. Smokestack education must give way to power learning.

The Passing of Smokestack Education

Back when factories provided the foundation for American success, schools delivered a curriculum to prepare most young people for spots on the assembly lines, a curriculum that stressed compliance, memorization, and scripts. A small percentage of the population was groomed for leadership by means of a tracking system that sorted and sifted students into levels of potential early in their school careers.

Today, the factory system of the 1950s and 1960s has moved off shore (Henkoff, 1992). Ours is an information-based and service economy that prizes flexibility, imagination, and innovation. Japan's success with total quality management has driven a movement to involve front-line workers in continuous improvement. What factory jobs remain increasingly depend on *informating*, a term coined by Shoshanna Zuboff to describe the powerful use of data to adjust production and service, as opposed to *automating*, which reduces procedures into relatively rigid computer programs (Zuboff, 1988).

The National Alliance of Business calls for workers with "the fourth 'R,' work force readiness, which includes reasoning, analytical, creative, and problem-solving skills, and behaviors such as reliability, responsibility, and responsiveness to new work requirements" (NAB, 1987, p. 1).

The Advent of Power Learning

Power learning encourages students to be *infotectives*. What is an *infotective*?—a student thinker capable of asking appropriate and powerful questions about *data* (with analysis) in order to convert the data into *information* (data organized so as to reveal patterns and relationships) and eventually into *insight* (information that may suggest action or strategy of some kind). An infotective solves information puzzles and riddles using all kinds of clues and new technologies. The problem solving that often follows the detective work then requires *synthesis* (invention) and *evaluation* (careful choices from lists of options). An infotective is a skilled thinker, researcher, and inventor.

Infotective is a term designed for education in the Information Age. In the smokestack school, teachers imparted meanings for students to digest, memorize, and regurgitate. In the Information Age school, students make the meaning. They puzzle their way through piles of fragments—sorting, sifting, weighing, and arranging them until a picture emerges.

New technologies enable even young students to test the power of relationships among variables in order to explore cause and effect and to attempt forecasting. These new technologies support hypothesis testing, theory testing, and model building by intermediate and middle school students as well as older ones. They allow systems thinking to creep down into elementary classrooms.

A turbulent, rapidly changing world confronts us with a great deal of non-sense, a swirling ocean of data bombarding the average citizen at a remarkable pace with an unrelenting intensity. Some of this data has been organized and manipulated in order to twist and control our thinking, as with political advertising, sound-bites, and infomercials. Toffler calls this manipulation *infotactics*. We need to raise a generation of infotectives who are capable of navigating through the oceans of data, even when the surface is heavy with fog, making sense out of non-sense and thereby building a healthier and stronger world community.

Power learning can produce a strong work force and a healthy, well-adjusted citizenry. Power learning addresses and imparts most of the skills identified as critical in studies such as "Workforce Basics: The Skills Employers Need"—basic skills, learning to learn, negotiating, self-esteem, career-planning, communicating, leadership, and creative problem solving (American Society for Training and Development [ASTD], 1988).

But power learning can also take children past work force and economic concerns to strengthen the social fabric, bolster the quality of life, and make productive citizenship a priority. We will expect students to act as "everyday heroes," by which Catford and

Ray (1991) mean that they will commit themselves to heroic, creative action, applying their new skills to improve life and to build a better community and world.

Power learning engages students in the use of new technologies along with what Catford and Ray identify as the four main tools of a hero: creative powers, careful observation, effective questioning, and an open mind. This book is designed to acquaint the reader with the wonderful marriage that is possible between power learning and these new technologies, touching on each of the major traditional subject areas and offering examples of classroom practice that puts students in the roles of thinker, researcher, and inventor.

Technology Snapshot 1.1

Half the fifth-graders in this classroom are busily programming turtles to follow their instructions on the screens of a dozen computer monitors, while the rest have spilled out into the hallway in pairs to connect LEGO™ pieces with electric motors, lights, wheels, and pulleys in an assortment of projects ranging from merry-go-rounds to assembly lines complete with light sensors. Their equipment assembled and wired, these young inventors step to the computer, plug in their devices, and call up a student-designed program that tells each device what to do.

An observer quickly notes the astute troubleshooting and the experimental flair of the group. If the device fails, the team immediately starts testing various hypotheses until the problem is solved. They seem reluctant to call on the teacher for help. Self-reliance and perseverance are alive and well.

Technology Snapshot 1.2

A group of middle school students gathers in the mayor's office to present their findings. One student moves forward to the overhead projector, adjusts the image on the LCD panel, and then clicks on a mouse to show their first colored graph.

"This graph shows you the fecal coliform content at various sites along Copper Creek," she explains. "Notice the sudden jump at site 5? Let me show you a map to help you relate to that location."

With another click of the mouse, the screen is filled with a close-up of a topographical map showing the meandering creek. In addition to the normal information found on such maps, this one also shows important structures along the path of the creek.

"You probably can see for yourself that a sewage treatment plant is located quite close to site 5, and because that belongs to the town, we are here to ask you to investigate the matter, to see if the plant is dumping raw sewage or something."

The mayor raises her eyebrows.

Conclusion

New technologies can allow us to revolutionize the way children learn about their world, significantly expanding the proportion of the citizenry that is capable of higher-level reasoning and imaginative problem solving. The key to successful implementation of such power learning programs is an understanding of the information skills that will be required by workers and citizens of the next century and of how technology plays a crucial role in enabling people to manage information. Even if we are preparing some students for jobs in factories, we must ask what kinds of factories these will be and what skills they will demand from their employees. Chances are that most jobs of the future will demand that employees be thinkers, researchers, and inventors capable of wielding technology in powerful ways.

Real-Time Research and Info Central

Because power learning engages students in "real-time research"—the exploration of essential questions using current data—schools must take a new look at their information resources and how they are networked to support this kind of research. Information Age schools modify libraries and media centers to coordinate the delivery of such information to learning locations, wherever they may be—home, classroom, field, or workplace.

Electronic highways will support research and thinking remote from the actual physical space occupied by the library itself but close to the learning action. Teachers and students will no longer need to delay or "send someone to the library" to find answers to pressing questions. Fresh, timely data will be right at hand.

Smokestack Research

A Scavenger Hunt

Smokestack education sees student research as a scavenger hunt in which students "go find out about" some topic, gathering up scraps of data and assorted findings. Such research is predominantly descriptive. Students collect what other people have thought and rearrange their findings in some kind of report. The process usually requires little independent reasoning.

Topical Research

One failing of smokestack research is a reliance on lists of topics rather than essential questions. In studying foreign countries, for example, students are often given a list of countries and a list of information categories, such as climate, raw materials, products, and culture. Invariably, students go to a library, pull out an encyclopedia article or a book about the country, and begin to transfer information from those printed materials to index cards or note paper. The trouble with this kind of research is its focus on the location and moving of information rather than the analysis of information. Again, little reasoning is required.

Value of Essential Questions

It would be far more productive, challenging, and intriguing to structure research projects around essential and higher-level questions, ones that require a good deal of student reasoning and probably cannot be answered by copying anybody else's thinking. In the case of foreign country studies, for example, students could be asked to identify the most pressing problems facing their assigned country and evaluate the likelihood that government initiatives are likely to fix those problems. They could be asked to speculate regarding the relationship between the rate of infant mortality and various health policies.

Questions requiring analysis, synthesis, and evaluation radically shift the research experience from descriptive, in which students mainly collect data, to explanatory, in which students try to gain insight from the data regarding important relationships. Power learning shows students how to build their own higher-level-thinking questions around the topics being studied by the class so that student research is tied both to the curriculum and to their personal curiosity.

Archaic Information Resources

But even if students are researching essential questions, smoke-stack schools often offered limited and archaic information re-sources. Conduct a study of the foreign country books in most school libraries, for example, and it is not unusual to find that the great majority of books are more than 10 years old.

In smokestack schools, students might study countries that no longer exist or study data and images of the country from time past. How many school libraries have a collection of books de-scribing the nations emerging from the former Soviet Union? This problem is not the fault of the librarian; it is the fault of the tech-nology. It is too costly for a librarian, or a publisher, to keep revis-ing such print resources.

Poor Information-Seeking Systems

A third flaw of the smokestack library is awkward systems for locating information—wooden boxes with cards inside, printed bibliographies, or the *Reader's Guide to Periodical Literature.* Index-ing systems rarely permit powerful search strategies involving combinations of key issues. If a student is studying the impact of one politician on the campaign of another, for example, there is no way to know which information resources will be right on target. Smokestack indexing condemns students to top-level categories and blocks the deeper mining of the resources.

With today's information technologies we can do an on-line word search through 36 newspapers from across the nation to find in less than a minute all articles mentioning Robert Reich, Bill Clinton, and the 1992 presidential election in the same paragraph. This type of search technology supports far more complex reason-ing about relationships and places the emphasis on reasoning rather than on locating.

Lack of Accessibility

Even those schools that view the library as the center of school learning still suffer from the physical limitations and scheduling realities of information resources being located remote from the learning action—unless students actually visited the library. In many schools and programs, research is a carefully orchestrated annual event rather than a daily treat. Intriguing questions arising during class discussion can rarely be answered on the spot. Fortunately, electronic highways will eventually link all students and teachers with information resources wherever they may be, and handheld "personal assistants" such as Apple's Newton™ may even support networking without wiring so that accessibility will be constant and independent of location.

Info Central: Tomorrow's Library Today

If we intend to make student research a daily part of the school experience, thus empowering reasoning about complex data, we must engage in *infotecture*—designing school information systems to deliver current data wherever and whenever students may have questions. Real-time research requires a fresh look at media centers and libraries as units coordinating "take out" information feasts. We will no longer judge the quality of a library by the number of books housed on its shelves. The test of a library will be the richness of the collection, the freshness of the data, its connectedness with external collections, and the ease with which students can gain access regardless of location. We might even take a few lessons from the pizza delivery business. We want information that is hot, fresh, and spicy delivered to our doorsteps in the wink of an eye.

Types of Data

A library once concentrated on print resources. The name changed to *media center* several decades ago as collections of tapes and videos arrived. Now the categories of data are expanding further, the modes of use are changing, and the name must change again—perhaps to *Info Central*. The library of tomorrow will have a great variety of resources ranging from artifacts, tape recordings, newspapers, magazines, and books to videodiscs containing thousands of photographs or paintings, CD-ROM discs holding hundreds of pages of text, databases offering numerical data or photographic collections, and on-line connections tying the school to just about every public information resource available throughout the world. It is likely that electronic information, digitized graphics, and hypertext will come to occupy an increasingly prominent place in this library because of their freshness, their ease of access, and the powerful tools such as statistical packages now available to probe such data.

Window to the World

Info Central will offer electronic field trips to students intent on understanding the world outside the classroom and the school. By tying into the national and global electronic highways now coming available (such as Internet), the school library can help all students venture out into that world without even leaving their classroom seats. Instead of the classroom being a student's world, the world will become the classroom.

On-line searches will put students in touch with the world's newspapers and databases, will open the doors of the world's museums, will give them access to the photographer's latest work, and will then support the quick transfer and downloading of such data into student computers for analysis and consideration.

Less costly searches will be conducted on resources resident in the library itself—CD-ROM disc towers offering thousands of pages of less current newspapers and journals, for example, which can be searched powerfully and inexpensively without paying for telecommunications charges.

Electronic Catalog

Info Central will offer an electronic catalog of its resources that can be searched at terminals in the library or remotely, and many of those resources will be available for home or class delivery. Unlike the card catalog, this electronic catalog will support far more powerful searches through descriptors attached to each resource. Students will be able to jump quickly to the section of a book that details Martin Luther King's last conversation with Malcolm X, for example, and download just those paragraphs that relate to the essential question being explored.

Information Shopping Center

Despite the current fascination with longer school years and school days as possible solutions to disappointing school performance, the school of the future is likely to reduce the number of hours of formal contact time between students and teachers as students engage in more research, both singly and in teams. The school library may become a community learning center where people of all ages may shop for information, stopping or plugging into a variety of information "boutiques." Virtual reality may become the school version of the shopping mall cinema, allowing students to "suit up" for thousands of exploits and adventures. Just as the *Jason Project* allows thousands of students to "be there" as a tele-presence at the floor of the ocean, virtual reality may transport students to settings hitherto unimaginable (Ballard, 1992).

Paintings and Hardcovers

Along with the dazzling new information technologies, the library will continue to offer archives of printed, nonelectronic media, such as copies of famous paintings and hard-covered novels with which to curl up in a corner. We must be careful to hold on to the best of the old technologies and exercise caution about what is lost with the new technologies. Some musicians, for example, have derided the loss of certain frequencies when music is recorded onto CD discs. They have claimed that a good deal of the emotion or soul of a piece may be lost with this technology that produces sound that is brighter than it is deep. The same is true for electronic versions of paintings by the great masters. Neither a paper print or a videodisc image of Van Gogh's paintings of irises can match the originals, but they each serve well until the student can manage a trip to the Metropolitan Museum in New York, the Getty Museum in Malibu, or the Van Gogh Museum in Amsterdam.

From Librarian to Information Importer/Exporter

The role of the librarian as media specialist will shift to include a major emphasis on infotecture—the design of information sharing systems across the school community. Although a premium will still be placed on creating an attractive and welcoming space to support research, the library program will become ubiquitous, omnipresent, and far-reaching. School librarians will oversee the electronic highways and make sure the information goods can flow smoothly to their appropriate markets.

Personal Assistants Linking Students to Info Central

Within the next few years, handheld personal assistants will allow students to communicate with Info Central without bothering to plug in or hook up—no matter where they are. Once this capability exists, libraries that stick to the smokestack mold may suddenly find themselves shut down by competitors beaming info-services down via cable, satellite, or some other vehicle. Now is the time to develop a local vision that will support a local facility carefully customizing its services to make it uniquely attractive to local populations. Otherwise, school libraries could go the way of "Mom and Pop" stores driven from business by supermarkets and huge discount stores. Perhaps the convenience stores that have spread rapidly across the nation in the past decade offer a model for Info Central.

Technology Snapshot 2.1

When asked to compare and contrast the impact of various writers during the 1840s, students in Council Rock, Pennsylvania, can turn to their Winnebago on-line catalog and search the collection by names and dates. A list soon flashes onto their screens that includes many resources that they might have "overlooked" in the past, collections of brief biographies or histories in which these people figured prominently enough for their names to appear in a descriptor field, as well as many documents available from other libraries in the region, such as the community college and the public libraries.

Technology Snapshot 2.2

A team of high school students evaluating the effectiveness of the Clean Air Act of 1990 in reducing problems of acid rain gathers around an IBM PC in the back of their classroom and calls up the *Reader's Guide Abstracts Select Edition,* a CD-ROM disc indexing and abstracting 25,000 selected articles each year from 237 core periodicals. Sitting in the CD-ROM tower of the school media center, this Wilsondisc™ provides the students with access to over 100,000 abstracts since 1988, and they need not even leave their classroom. Applying the Boolean logic search strategies they have been taught, they quickly generate a list of relevant articles and begin assigning portions of the list for home reading, since each member of the team can dial in to the school media center at night from home and download the articles he or she wishes to read.

Conclusion

School information services are undergoing a remarkable transformation in those districts where the librarians or media specialists have ventured out onto the leading edge by exploring ways to bring the best information services of the adult workplace into the schools. In such districts, students find themselves immersed in data and information resources that are far richer and more accessible than those provided by smokestack schools. Because power learning, which dramatically increases the responsibility of students to generate insight from data, depends on rich resources freely, easily, and widely available, the shift to Info Central and its powerful connection with electronic highways is a keystone in the development of schools for the Information Age.

High-Tech Social Studies

S ocial studies offers fertile ground for power learning. Whether in history, geography, or the social sciences, the importance of sifting through data to gain insight is paramount. New technologies enrich the data available to students while eliminating many of the frustrations that have blocked students from mining primary sources in the past.

Regrettably, studies of social studies classroom practice have documented a long-standing preoccupation with lecture and memorization. Smokestack education has found one of its most solid and loyal followers in this discipline. At the same time, there has always been a minority of social studies educators who have emphasized inquiry and the use of primary sources to empower student thinking, an approach well suited to the new technologies (Morrissett, 1981).

Perhaps as a consequence of archaic methodologies and a national emphasis on other subject areas, studies of student knowledge, skills, and attitudes in the social studies point to serious problems and gaps. Put simply, the typical 11th-grader doesn't know much about the world, including where things are and how things work. This same student has trouble demonstrating the kinds of reasoning required for decision making in a democracy and lacks basic attitudes, such as tolerance of diversity, that keep the society healthy. In short, citizenship and social studies education (which includes history, geography, and the social sciences) have long been in a state of decline (Martin, 1980). New technologies could do a great deal to breathe life into this slumbering giant.

Charting a Course for the 21st Century

Charting a Course: Social Studies for the 21st Century clarifies the historical, geographic, political, social, and cultural knowledge required for good citizenship. The social studies curriculum should enable students to develop the following:

1. Civic responsibility and active civic participation.
2. Perspectives on their own life experiences so they see themselves as part of the larger human adventure in time and place.
3. A critical understanding of the history; geography; economic, political, and social institutions; traditions; and values of the United States as expressed in both their unity and their diversity.
4. An understanding of other peoples and the unity and diversity of world history, geography, institutions, traditions, and values.
5. Critical attitudes and analytical perspectives appropriate to analysis of the human condition. (NCSS, 1989, p. 6)

In identifying essential characteristics of a social studies curriculum for the 21st century, three sections speak especially well to the contributions that may be made with new technologies (NCSS, 1989, p. 3):

First, content knowledge from the social studies should not be treated merely as received knowledge to be accepted and memorized but as the means through which open and vital questions may be explored and confronted. Students must be made aware that just as contemporary events have been shaped by actions taken by people in the past, they themselves have the capacity to shape the future.

Second, reading, writing, observing, debating, role-playing (or simulations), working with statistical data, and using appropriate critical thinking skills should be an integral part of social studies instruction. Teaching strategies should help students to become both independent and cooperative learners who develop skills of problem solving, decision making, negotiation, and conflict resolution.

Third, learning materials must incorporate a rich mix of written matter, including original sources, literature, and expository writing; a variety of audiovisual materials, including films, television, and interactive media; a collection of items of material culture, including artifacts, photographs, census records, and historical maps; and computer programs for writing and analyzing social, economic, and geographic data. Social studies coursework should teach students to evaluate the reliability of all such sources of information and to be aware of the ways in which various media select, shape, and constrain information.

Mining the Mountain

Megatrends was one of the first books to identify the challenge accompanying the vast information resources now available (Naisbitt, 1982). Today's students have millions of pages of text and thousands of pictures at their fingertips. A click of the mouse opens up a mountain range of documents holding rich veins of meaning below the surface. The danger lies in the enormity and complexity of the task. How does one mine these resources, probing below the surface to find the data relevant to the questions being explored? How does one avoid drowning or choking on *info-glut*? New data sources such as videodiscs, CD-ROM, and on-line databases can illuminate student research questions, but only if the students know how to navigate and find their way below the surface.

The social studies teacher of today and tomorrow becomes less of an expert and more of a guide, showing students the skills that empower them to sort and sift through these resources on the way to making meaning. Such skills require elimination of the barriers that have long stood between school disciplines, as mathematical reasoning becomes an essential partner in the search for meaning in social studies, for example. If students gather data, they must know how to explore the significance of relationships between various variables, a reasoning task that involves statistical inference. They must also know ways to judge the reliability of the data.

In the smokestack era, students were warned not to believe everything they read in newspapers or books. Today we must warn them not to believe everything they read, see, or hear in various databases and collections. Survey data, for example, may lead to invalid conclusions because items were phrased in a biased manner. Students must weigh the data after they collect it, asking how it was gathered and whether or not it can be trusted.

Toffler warns that powerful figures intentionally manipulate data in order to sway people's thinking, using *info-tactics* and *meta-tactics* to cast a desirable light on a particular decision or to cover disturbing phenomena with fog. He points out that one must travel back to examine the assumptions built into the data collection and track how those assumptions might have distorted the findings, because info-tacticians usually try to hide these assumptions while emphasizing findings or conclusions (Toffler, 1990).

Social studies teachers can best prepare students to challenge such faulty thinking in two ways: (1) engaging them in their own research projects, which acquaints them with research design issues, and (2) involving them in critiques of flawed studies. The goal is the development of *info-skepticism,* a healthy tendency to look past other people's insights to detect bias and distortion. The shift is from consumption of others' insights to production of one's own insight.

To prevent *info-paralysis,* teachers must show students how to employ powerful search strategies. This involves acquainting the students with: (1) the structure of databases so they know where to look, (2) Boolean logic (the use of various connecting words or range indicators, such as *and, or,* and >) so they can identify relevant records, and (3) the creation of powerful questioning techniques that will enable them to carve through the mountain.

In designing such learning experiences, teachers must provide a range of activities that introduce students to visual and numerical data as well as text. Full information literacy includes all kinds of data. Thus students must learn to analyze photography, television coverage, and various forms of advertising critically. Mary Alice White argues that even though students will learn more than half of what they know about the world through visual data, few schools have an explicitly stated curriculum dedicated toward teaching students *visual literacy* —the ability to apply critical thinking to visual data and images (White, 1984). Because visual data is especially susceptible to the use of info-tactics in the war to win the minds (and the votes) of the citizenry, social studies teachers have a particular responsibility in this regard.

Technology Snapshot 3.1

Fifth-graders work as two-person teams with a user-friendly database program that allows them to scan through records on various kinds of information treasure hunts. Today's worksheet provides clues about presidents. Students must figure out which president was born in 1804, served in the Navy, and was a senator before election to the presidency. At first they click through every record until they stumble on the right birthdate. They then check to see if the rest of the clues match. It is a slow process, but they enjoy being infotectives.

Wanting her students to see the powers of computer searching, the teacher circulates around the room and asks each team to command the computer to search for a particular date. In a few seconds, the target record stares them in the eye and their faces brighten with excitement.

Walking down the hall of this same school, one encounters computer-generated bar charts showing the results of a student survey for the upcoming 1996 presidential election. Once they learn how to use someone else's databases, they begin building their own databases to answer whatever questions are on their minds.

Technology Snapshot 3.2

On the day after the 1992 election, as an 11th-grade class sits discussing the results, one student blurts out a question about term limits.

"I don't understand," she says. "If people want term limits, why do they keep reelecting their own representatives?"

"They don't," argues a second student. "A whole bunch of incumbents lost last night."

"Like what percentage of the whole group?" asks the first girl.

The second student shrugs, confessing a lack of data.

"We could easily find out," interrupts the teacher, "by searching through the PAPERS™ database on DIALOG, which lets us scan 30 papers from around the nation. One of them must have reported that percentage."

"Yeah," chimes in a new student, "and we could even check to see which states had ballot questions on term limits and see how incumbents did in each of those states. That way we could check and see if the voters are saying one thing and doing the other."

The teacher begins a search on the PC in the front of the room to identify which states had ballot questions on term limits, and then the class is split into research teams, one for each selected state. Steering their PCs onto the electronic highway, each team calls up newspapers for their target state with the intention of finding data to report back to the whole group. One group is assigned to plan how a statistical package such as DataDesk™ can serve them to merge, analyze, and report the results of all the other groups' searching.

Technology Snapshot 3.3

Three students are spending the evening in Info Central exploring the question of what role charisma will play in Bill Clinton's presidency. They have already explored a dozen articles on charismatic leadership on previous visits, employing the CD-ROM towers, which put the wisdom of hundreds of historians, philosophers, political scientists, and pundits at their fingertips. Tonight they are looking back at previous presidents, concentrating on newsreel footage contained in the *Video Encyclopedia of the 20th Century*™. Their exploration tool is *The 20th Century Navigator*™, a HyperCard program allowing them to access reference and index materials for the 2300+ unit, 42-disc set.

"Let's replay Roosevelt's speech one more time . . . that one section about 'fear itself.' Watch his eyes and his face. Listen to his voice. Compare that with what we saw of Hoover earlier. I think he has some kind of magical touch that hits people in their gut. It reminds me of Clinton, but Clinton always seems to be trying too hard."

"Yeah, it's almost as if Clinton went back and watched these tapes to learn how to sway people, but he doesn't quite get it. It doesn't seem real. It's too slick, almost like makeup. I really wonder whether he'll be able to inspire people."

The first student clicks on the mouse and the videodisc player whirs. FDR's face comes into focus and his words flow.

"Let's save that segment for our visual essay. Just those 12 seconds. They illustrate really well what we've been finding out about hitting people in their gut."

Traveling the Electronic Highway

Telecommunications not only link students to powerful databases, they also serve to shrink the world by tying people together from many different states and nations using bulletin boards and E-mail of various kinds. As one more cure to the archaic data characteristic of smokestack social studies programs, this electronic highway supports the gathering of all kinds of fresh information by communicating directly with people who are close to whatever is being studied.

The quality and accuracy of optical character recognition software is improving, and we are moving to optical fiber support for the rapid transmission of graphics. These advances will improve the quality and quantity of data improve that can be exchanged as students from widely different locations share local newspaper stories, photographs, tourist guides, and all manner of documents.

In addition to the exchange of data, telecommunications could support a kind of international dialogue that may dramatically lower cultural barriers and bring about what the Global Business Network has called the "global teenager"—a generation tied together by a global culture created by electronic media (P. Schwartz, 1991). International exchange will no longer be limited to small cadres of visitors. Some students may elect to "visit" other countries daily, taking advantage of the electronic highway. Carefully guided by imaginative social studies teachers, these exchanges could do a great deal to advance world understanding while fueling here in the United States a resurgence of interest in learning foreign languages, including those of the Far East as well as those of Europe.

Microworlds, Tele-Presence, and Virtual Reality

New technologies will provide students with vicarious experience that will sometimes seem more real than the actual event might. The quality of computer simulations keeps improving as multimedia adds dimensions and senses to the mix, and we are moving toward virtual reality programs for schools that will provide electronic field trips, expeditions, excursions, treks, and adventures to far distant lands and times.

Tom Snyder Productions offers a whole series of simulations entitled Decisions, Decisionsœ, which place students in group problem-solving situations related to their social studies or science curriculum: *Colonization, Revolutionary Wars, Immigration, Urbanization, Foreign Policy, Television, The Budget Process, On the Campaign Trail, The Environment, Prejudice,* and *Substance Abuse.*

Project Jason now brings thousands of students to the bottom of the sea through the magic of *tele-presence. Palenqué* allows students to "walk" through Mayan ruins. *Simcity* involves them in running a city. Before long students may be able to sit as judges in the Salem witch trials or at Nuremburg, making important decisions and seeing their consequences. They may be able to visit Gettysburg and join Pickett's ill-fated charge. Hopefully, most of these programs will provide opportunities to "help students become both independent and cooperative learners who develop skills of problem-solving, decision-making, negotiation and conflict resolution" (NCSS, 1989, p. 19). Virtual reality may help to bring social studies to life, engaging students in role-playing with more vitality and passion than was previously possible.

It is important to note that virtual reality does have its limitations and its dangers. Because simulations are oversimplified models of reality, students must be taught to see how they differ from reality so they do not become prey to "virtual truth" or "virtual thought." As Postman warns in *Technopoly*, when the phone company asks us to "reach out and touch someone," we must never forget the difference between tele-touch and human touch (Postman, 1992). A tele-presence on the bottom of the ocean is very different from a real presence, just as acting the role of judge on a computer falls far short of what it must have really been. Power learning exploits these differences, heightening the student's understanding of the real thing by critiquing the simulation's inadequacies and strengths.

Conclusion

New technologies offer social studies educators a powerful array of tools with which to achieve the laudable goals established by the National Council of the Social Studies. Power learning develops citizens who are prepared to tackle the baffling and bewildering questions and issues facing an Information Age society. Although the use of such technologies represents a major break with past traditions, the importance of the task and the need for such a break is underlined by repeatedly disappointing evaluations of current student knowledge and skill levels.

High-Tech Math and Science

In 1989, revolutionary reports published by leaders of both mathematics education and science education called for fundamental shifts in the way our students learn math and science. Technology promises to play a prominent role in the implementation of the curriculum standards of the National Council of Teachers of Mathematics (NCTM) and the recommendations of *Science for All Americans: Summary, Project 2061*. As this book went to press, the National Academy of Sciences was unveiling principles for science standards similar to the NCTM standards.

Full coverage of these two proposals lies outside the scope of this book, but this chapter will focus on several themes that are especially ripe for support from technology. This chapter also treats the two disciplines together, for that is a major recommendation of both groups that students should experience the two in tandem, each serving the other to help explore and explain the world.

The themes of Project 2061 include an emphasis on systems, models, constancy, patterns of change, evolution, and scale. According to this report, teaching should start with questions about nature, engage students actively, concentrate on the collection and use of evidence, provide historical perspective, insist on clear expression, use a team approach, not separate knowing from finding out, and de-emphasize the memorization of technical vocabulary. It goes on to suggest that science teaching welcome curiosity, reward creativity, encourage a spirit of healthy questioning, avoid dogmatism, and promote aesthetic responses. Science teaching should aim to counteract learning anxieties. Science teaching should extend beyond the school and should take its time (American Association for the Advancement of Science [AAAS], 1989).

The NCTM standards likewise stress models, systems, the analysis and interpretation of data, and the use of statistical inference as applied to real-life situations. Mathematics is seen as delivering powerful support for the construction of meaning and the development of insight (Frye, 1989).

Systems, Simulation, and Statistical Inference

Most phenomena (physical or human) can be viewed as part of a *system*, with elements woven together in a more or less complex web of relationships. Science and mathematics help us understand how these elements interact. We build simplified versions of systems (called *models*), place them on computers (where they become *simulations*), and then explore what happens when we change any of the elements (called *variables*).

When students first start learning about systems with such models, they explore on the computer with commercially designed or teacher-invented simulations. Ultimately, we expect them to learn to construct their own models and simulations. The construction of a reasonably realistic model is convincing evidence of understanding on a very high level.

New technologies enable even young students to test the power of relationships between variables in order to explore cause and effect and to attempt forecasting. These new technologies support hypothesis testing, theory testing, and model building by intermediate and middle school students as well as the older ones. They allow systems thinking to creep down into elementary classrooms.

For most research questions, we are hoping to find out how something works in order to make wise decisions and solve various problems. The more we know about a system and how its key variables interact, so the theory goes, the more likely we are to act in ways that are fruitful.

In the early stages of learning about systems, the computer provides students with simulations that allow them to see the effect of changing one variable or another. This is called *parameter manipulation* (Mandinach & Cline, 1992a).

Intellimation's Physics Simulations

This package of physics simulations allows students to shoot off a piece of artillery over and over again without suffering powder burns, destroying the landscape, or hurting anybody's ears. The student can adjust the parameters of four different variables (velocity magnitude, angle, friction, and decay) and then fire off the ball to note the resulting trajectory, which is etched across the screen each time until cleared by the student. After 20 trials, there will be 20 trajectories showing. The visualization builds intuitive understanding that serves as a foundation for more formal mathematical and scientific reasoning.

STACI[N]

The Systems Thinking and Curriculum Innovation Network Project developed by ETS has been exploring the use of a software program called STELLA™, a simulation-modeling package, for six years with six high schools and two middle schools. The project results reported in studies have been dramatic (Mandinach & Cline, 1992a).

Crawford and Molder (1992) describe a STACI[N] teacher-designed middle school wolf project that bridges language arts, math, and science, involving students in a computer program written about wolves and predator/prey relationships.

Mandinach and Cline (1992a) identify four levels of systems thinking proceeding from the *parameter manipulation* described above to the construction of simplified models, called *constrained modeling*, to the development of more complex models, called *epitome modeling*, and finally, to the creation of *learning environments*. The higher up this ladder the student proceeds, the greater the understanding.

In addition to systems/modeling programs such as *STELLA*, today's infotectives will employ user-friendly statistical packages such as *PEMD Discovery*™ and *DataDesk*™ to support number crunching, picture making, and inference. After all, we know that "a picture is worth a thousand words." A graph is often the best way to communicate the meaning lying hidden in a scattering of thousands of datapoints.

PEMD Discovery

PEMD Education Group offers a CD-ROM disc called the *Environmental Data Disc* containing over 125 megabytes of data (such as temperature and precipitation data from over 800 U.S. stations; worldwide food, agricultural, and demographic data; economic and trade data; and much more) as well as a very user-friendly exploration tool called *Discovery*, which allows students to explore relationships between variables by graphing various combinations. The graphing process requires a simple click on a menu to designate the X- or Y-axis and then the selection of various data groups the student wishes to compare.

The student may use personally collected data (creating datastacks to fit an experiment, for example), may import data from already existing spreadsheets, or may rely on PEMD's CD-ROM data. In order to support topics of particularly strong current interest, PEMD provides learning modules on AIDS, CO_2 Emissions, Global Warming, Ozone, and Petroleum, setting up datastacks for students with all key relevant variables already established and the design of the datastack already done for the student. All the student has to do is start clicking and the graphs will pop onto the screen with amazing speed and clarity. Once the graphs appear, the student may change their scale, their color, and their size; stack them up; or tile them so that as many as eight graphs can all be seen at the same time.

Although *PEMD Discovery* is primarily visual, the data explored graphically in that program can also be exported to statistical packages such as *DataDesk* if one wishes to obtain correlations and other measures.

DataDesk

DataDesk is a statistical package from Data Descriptions, Inc. with a visual emphasis. It is capable of performing all of the statistical calculations you might wish to perform with a database, but it goes much further by providing many different forms of display, many of which can be adjusted and manipulated to explore relationships visually.

Calculations
- Correlations (Pearson Product Moment, Kendall's tau, Spearman Rank Correlation, Covariance)
- Regression
- ANOVA
- Cluster Analysis
- Frequency Breakdowns
- Contingency Tables

Displays
- Histograms
- Bar Charts
- Pie Charts
- Scatterplots
- Rotation Plot
- Dotplots
- Boxplots
- Lineplots

After students enter or import data from science or social studies projects, *DataDesk* allows them to explore mathematical relationships between whatever variables they select and to see what they look like.

Technology Snapshot 4.1

One science teacher whose students had collected and recorded water samples from various sites along a community stream for over 20 years was able to enter into *DataDesk* more than a dozen measurements, such as fecal coliform content and pH, from a half-dozen sites along the stream with the samples being repeated hourly through the night for 10 times. The total datapoints exceeded 14,000—a true data gold mine.

Once data for the 20 years were entered, each succeeding year was far less work, but the potential for insight was remarkable and the extracting of rich relationships was quite easy.

To see the pattern of fecal coliform content from site to site down the stream this year, the student highlights the right dates, clicks on the "time" field to designate it as the X-axis, and then clicks on fecal content as the Y-axis—the variable being graphed. The computer then draws the line or bar graph in just a few seconds, in color if wished. Repeat the process for each of the previous years and the screen fills with 19 more graphs. One can see the gradual pollution of the stream, pinpoint its zenith, and locate the most likely origin.

Because of its emphasis on visual displays and the many tools provided to adjust those visual displays, *DataDesk* supports student exploration of mathematical relationships without requiring understanding of graduate-school-level statistical formulas and concepts.

Correlations, for example, can make sense to upper elementary students without their understanding the mathematical procedures required to calculate them. In the case of the stream mentioned above, it takes a few moments to create scatterplots charting combinations of measures such as pH and fecal coliform content. If they are strongly related to each other, they will cluster close to the diagonal. One can see it clearly. But if one wants to know the actual correlation, it is a simple matter of clicking on a menu. Seconds later you have the relationship confirmed or denied. It is not difficult for a 5th- or 6th-grader to learn the difference between a correlation of .90 and one of .50.

Traveling the Electronic Highway

The electronic highway linking students from around the world in information hunting and gathering can have a positive impact on social policies by spotlighting issues. Some problems such as the disposal of hazardous waste were once sustained by the lack of exposure and disclosure, but students who are committed to a healthy planet may begin to employ new technologies to bring dangerous and harmful practices out into the open, identifying sources of pollution along community streams and joining with students in other towns, states, and nations to establish data collections that will reveal significant regional patterns and help pinpoint trouble spots.

Students across the world may become skilled environmental trouble-spotters. Students may employ their scientific technology skills in combination with their telecommunication skills to provide the globe with an environmental alert. Once they see the patterns, they may wish to act as infotectives, hypothesizing as to why certain variations may occur in their locations and then checking their hypotheses using the four tools of the hero mentioned in Chapter 1: creative powers, observation, questioning, and an open mind. Trained in systems thinking, they are careful to look at the big picture, identifying all key elements that might have a significant influence on the patterns they are studying.

The electronic highway supports a new kind of global student community that trades stories, tricks of the trade, and strategies as well as information. A cry for help posted on a bulletin board may attract several dozen helpful suggestions. The isolation of the smokestack science lab with its inclined planes and gas burners is replaced by a science program that is inclined to social action, employing science in the service of the community. Students stop asking, "Why do we have to learn this stuff?"

Opening the Information Window

Students now have extraordinary information resources available to them. In addition to sources such as the videodiscs, CD-ROM discs, and on-line databases mentioned in Chapter 3, young scientists can also test their "What if?" questions with hardware and software designed to be used in the classroom science lab. The software may serve to increase the amount of hands-on science in many schools by eliminating dangers, difficulties, and time constraints.

IBM's *Personal Science Laboratory (PSL)*, for example, offers probes that can measure such variables as temperature, light intensity, voltage, pH, distance, and force. As the students work with these probes, the software collects data, stores it in a data table, and plots datapoints on a graph. Students are provided with "real-time graphing," seeing the results of their experiment on screen as it is conducted. The software also offers data manipulation and analysis tools to help students discover relationships among the data after it has been collected and stored.

Teachers have reported that because this technology relieves students from the tedium of data collection, it frees them to concentrate on the meaning of the data. They praise the speed and accuracy of the data collection process and indicate that students were given a greater opportunity to explore relationships between variables (IBM, 1992).

A number of Level III videodisc programs (those using computer software to drive the videodisc player) involve students in problem-solving scenarios. In *ErgoMotion*™, for example, a program offered by Houghton Mifflin, students learn how the laws of physics affect everyday life, redesigning a roller coaster in one activity and seeing how physics affects its design. In *Science Sleuths*™, a Videodiscovery program utilizing barcodes, students solve open-ended scientific mysteries such as why the lawn mowers are exploding in one housing development, navigating through a variety of documents and visual resources on the videodisc.

The availability of videodisc-based science programs keeps growing as Optical Data Corporation has state approval in Texas for its Windows™ program and Texas Learning Technology Group (TLTG) is close behind them with the development of a middle school program.

In order to make power learning a reality in the science classroom, we must take a careful look at the tools we place in the hands of our students and ask to what extent they mirror the kinds of tools being used by practicing scientists. Meeting the national educational goals in science requires a substantial shift in practice to bring school science into alignment with real world science.

Learning Teams

Many educators are concerned about the isolating effects of students working long hours on computers, but collaborative problem solving can thrive in a high technology context so long as students are assigned to work in teams. The experimental nature of the activity keeps curiosity and task commitment high while the shared screen seems to help provide focus and structure. One benefit of these new technologies may be the cooperative learning that will result from teachers moving off stage to support more student-centered learning and research.

Seeing Is Believing—and Understanding

Those science programs that hitherto relied almost exclusively on textbooks often met with difficulty trying to inspire student enthusiasm for science while explaining complex concepts. With the advent of videodisc-based science programs, the teacher can have thousands of illustrations, slides, charts, graphs, drawings, and models close at hand to make science more appetizing and more comprehensible.

Because each videodisc can hold some 54,000 pictures on each side and because the computer software knows how to reach any one picture in a second or two, the teacher can conduct lessons with great flexibility and power. Because the software programs driving such videodiscs usually permit word searches, teacher and class can navigate through the 54,000 pictures with efficiency and save the results of the search in whatever sequence they wish for later viewing.

In addition to still pictures, most videodisc programs also offer brief video segments to illustrate such phenomena as a heart beating under a variety of conditions (for example, the use of stimulants). Unlike the VCR, the videodisc player supports very careful analysis of such material. Each frame (moving normally at 30 frames per second) can be frozen in place without damaging the disc. One can adjust the speed, backward and forward, to half a dozen speeds. Because each frame has a number assigned to it, it is possible to return to a section of the video in less than 2 seconds without rewinding. Slowing the video down and looking frame by frame radically changes what students see and understand. It is also possible to leap into a different unit's pictures to explore relationships between shared concepts, moving back and forth between earthquakes and volcanoes, for example.

Conclusion

In recent decades, the percentage of students showing interest in math or science careers has declined dramatically (Jones, 1992). Given the extensive impact that math, science, and technology will all have on the society of the next century, we cannot afford a generation that is illiterate in or alienated from any of these disciplines. As with social studies, new technologies promise to set math and science instruction free from their smokestack limitations, making them both more enjoyable, enlightening, and helpful to students trying to make sense of their worlds.

One expects that the infotectives emerging from this kind of math and science experience will possess the ability to achieve insight as they proceed through life—insight to guide voting, career selection, and a contribution to society. Rather than being befuddled by infomercials and propaganda about global warming and the ozone layer, they will puzzle their way out of the forest, using systems thinking to climb a tree and see the forest and its pathways. Shown a series of graphs, they will ask what models lie behind the pictures—and what assumptions are hidden below the surface. At a time when technology promises much, either in the way of destruction or progress, the path we end up selecting is more likely to be a healthy one if we have citizens capable of asking such questions while employing scientific and mathematical reasoning.

High-Tech English

In smokestack schools, students are primarily consumers of others' ideas and insights. They are expected to swallow what they read more or less whole in the order of courses presented: appetizers first, dessert last. In the Information Age school, as students will be producing ideas, they will be engaged in understanding how ideas are put together—how they are structured—and they will be making up their own minds. Because electronic text makes it easy to do, they will learn to hop, skip, and jump—mentally.

New technologies promise to change many of the ways we speak, write, listen, think, and understand. Some of these changes will be beneficial, contributing to power learning of the kind described in previous chapters. These changes may strengthen the reasoning powers of students, helping them to become thinkers, researchers, and inventors. They may also support the development of poetic, intuitive, and multisensory capabilities.

However, we must also be on the lookout for ways that technologies may undermine those same possibilities, bearing in mind Postman's (1992) charge that technology, blindly accepted, is a form of cultural AIDS, undermining our belief systems and key cultural values in subtle ways.

This chapter explores changing conceptions of what it means to read, write, and communicate in the Information Age, given the arrival of electronic, digitized information. The essential question is how the new technologies can best be employed in schools to achieve power learning.

What It Now Means to Read

Electronic Text—Key to Open-Minded Thinking

When the printing press made the printed word available to the middle classes and, ultimately, to the entire citizenry, it helped to create a social revolution that led to the decline of monarchy and the rise of democracy in the Western world. Ideas and information could no longer be suppressed or monopolized. Electronic text— because of its permeability, fluidity, malleability, responsiveness, availability, transportability, and marriageability—may have an equally momentous impact on the nature of society, actually supporting the growth of open-minded thinking and collaboration in a culture that has long tended toward closed-mindedness and argumentation.

The Printed Word—Lockstep Reasoning

Most of us learned to read the printed page from left to right and from top to bottom. When reading a book, we usually began on the first page and kept turning pages until we found our way to the back. Reading has long been very sequential. Most of us have accepted the structure offered by the author. We assume that the first paragraph is first for a very good reason, and the same for the second paragraph. Sentences, paragraphs, and chapters are laid out in a sequence carefully orchestrated by the writer, who, we assume, has a plan in mind for how we might best learn whatever message is being expressed. How many readers began this book, for example, by skimming the final chapter?

In smokestack classrooms, even though some models of reading did encourage scanning and questioning prior to reading (S3QR, for example), students were rarely encouraged to break the sequential pattern. Even those models were limited by human technology—the eye as a scanner. The reader could search only as far as the eye could see. The sheer volume of words and pages in a history book made searching for ideas difficult and very time-consuming. Back in the 1950s and 1960s, many people paid for speed-reading courses that taught how to skim through text and focus on main ideas, but the path remained quite linear.

Student as Consumer of Ideas

The main purpose for much of the nonfiction reading in smokestack schools was the consumption of the author's ideas and evidence. Once the ideas had been consumed and committed to memory, the student would be expected to regurgitate, either reciting the lessons in class or on some test. Even when handling questions at the top of *Bloom's Taxonomy*, many students were encouraged to borrow the thinking of experts, citing them carefully in footnotes.

Judging from discouraging NAEP data on critical thinking skills possessed by 11th-graders in reading (less than 10% of the students demonstrate high skill), few students have been engaged in analyzing the logic and the structure of authors' ideas, a deficit that also shows up when it comes to students' ability to edit their own writing to improve reasoning as well as expression (Applebee et al., 1986).

Printed Text—The Constraints of Linearity

The main premise of this chapter is that the linearity of printed text lends itself especially well to student consumption of others' ideas. The job of the student with pre-electronic texts is to "follow" and learn the authors' thinking. Electronic text makes it much easier for the student to explore and critique the thinking of others on the way to producing her or his own insights.

Electronic Text—Permeable

Unlike printed text in books, electronic text is extremely easy to penetrate. One can probe below the surface to find previously elusive ideas or facts with ease. We can now retrieve the proverbial needle in the haystack in a matter of seconds. This permeability means that it is much easier to explore other people's thinking, maintain an open mind, and draw one's own conclusions. It is easier to play around with the pieces of some mental puzzle.

Whereas printed text is somewhat like a very long necklace with its beads (thoughts and evidence) sequentially strung, electronic text is more like a wonderful stew pot simmering on the stove. When you lift off the lid, you may stir and ladle up what suits your taste in whatever order you wish, especially if you have been trained to understand how ideas may fit together.

Because of this permeability, reading in the Information Age will come to include a more inventive, less sequential approach to exploring the content of a text file. Our students will become skilled browsers and seekers. They will be infoctectives—modern diviners wielding electronic magic wands. It is almost as if we had taken the beads off the string so we can turn them into dozens of new necklaces. Other people's ideas are suddenly in the service of each student's individual thinking.

Electronic Text—Fluid

Unlike printed text in books, electronic text is extremely easy to move around. Employing various cut-and-paste functions, the reader can rearrange the information and the idea, combining it with information and ideas gleaned from other texts. These combinations will often spawn new ideas. Whereas the linearity of print restricted rearrangement and idea play, the fluidity of electronic text invites such play.

As a result of searching through text files, reading will come to include some form of collecting and storing of thoughts. The reader will want to store bits and pieces, like shells found along the seashore or like beads unstrung from a necklace, in ways that will allow them to be retrieved or revisited for play and consideration. Fortunately, the new technologies offer dynamic, relational databases supporting inventive and imaginative searching of such thought treasure chests.

Information Age readers will know how to conduct the following kinds of searches, plus some new kinds not yet invented: user-defined concept searches, nested (progressive) searches, fuzzy searches (word roots), field or block searches, vocabulary list (browse index) searches, phonetic searches, and thesaurus or synonym searches. They will also be skilled at creating links to structure their treasure chest for future searching: interdocument links, bookmarks, notes attached to text, and tables of contents (Ga Coté & Diehl, 1992). Various artificial intelligence systems will prompt readers in both searching and structuring. "Have you thought about adding articles from the following related concepts?"

Electronic Text—Malleable

Unlike printed text in books, electronic text is extremely easy to modify. The infotective can substitute new elements, combine elements, expand or compress elements, change the sequence, eliminate elements, and reverse elements. Such malleability invites open-minded thinking. The mind is not set like concrete; we can entertain new ideas and see how they dovetail with the ideas we already hold.

Electronic Text—Responsive

Unlike printed text in books, electronic text almost seems conversant, changing on the screen before our eyes as we ask questions and probe below the surface. Our queries create a kind of electronic dialogue. As artificial intelligence modules evolve, we will have a personal assistant such as Apple's Newton giving us prompts in the form of questions or menus to help us with the inquiry and exploration.

Stymied, confused, or lost in the maze of text, Information Age students will learn to trust their personal assistants to act as guides in some cases, suggesting ways out of their quandaries, but it will be a two-way street. They will also train the personal assistant as they proceed and their thinking matures. Student and personal assistant will grow together along with a vast information storage system filled with hypertext far beyond the retention capacity of the human brain but intricately and powerfully linked to the team-thinking of student and personal assistant.

Electronic Text—Available

Unlike printed text in books, electronic text is very easy to locate and physically possess. Imagine if someone asked 20 years ago for the text from the day's front page of 25 leading newspapers. It might take days to obtain the actual papers. Otherwise, in order to meet the deadline, one could call the 25 newspapers long distance and ask them to read their front pages over the phone while a secretary transcribed the dictation.

Today, one can conduct a simple database search and have the documents downloaded in less than an hour. As information centers around the world come to be linked through Internet and other networks, the average reader will be able to access mega-tomes of information cheaply, quickly, and powerfully. With the marketing of CD-ROM readers to the home market, electronic books have become a reality, with a single disc offering thousands of pages of books and documents.

Electronic Text—Transportable

Unlike printed text in books, electronic text can be exchanged, shared, and transmitted with great facility, speed, and economy. If one buys a best-selling book in a hardcover edition, sharing with friends must wait until one finishes the book and passes it along—unless one is comfortable with oral readings or friends peering over one's shoulder. Having typed a single memo to 50 classmates with a question about a passage in a French newspaper just downloaded the same morning, the student may send memo and article out to all 50 students over an electronic mail network in less time than it would have taken previously to mail it to one student using "snail mail." Electronic information resources move around with great rapidity. Because they are transportable, their impact can grow exponentially, although electronic posting does not guarantee reading or comprehending at the other end.

Electronic Text—Marriageable

Unlike printed text in books, electronic text files and resources can be linked in dynamic ways that cross what used to be information barriers or boundaries. If all of Shakespeare's works appear on one CD-ROM disc, for example, it becomes possible to identify and store every example of his use of the word *woman* from across all the plays and poems. Stored as fragments of text, brief quotations, "keywords in context," these items can be merged with a similar collection from Hemingway and the resulting compendium can be reshuffled, sorted, and analyzed with great power.

Implications for Schools

It becomes difficult to separate electronic reading from thinking. It turns out that they are close relatives. We scan words and search for information in order to change our thinking, to learn something new, to gain insight. Even though some students and adults have been doing this kind of thinking long before the arrival of electronic text, electronic text makes it natural, increases its power dramatically, and makes it available to those who might not otherwise think this way.

For those concerned about the slipping rank of the United States on various international student tests and our apparent lack of progress on national educational goals, it stands to reason that America's continued leadership in the world might be assured by moving quickly to take advantage of hypertext as a way of promoting student reasoning, creating a nation of Toffler's brainworkers capable of making up their own minds.

What It Means to Write

The new technologies have also radically changed writing, mostly for the better.

In smokestack schools, writing was often confused with the process of putting words down on paper in the same structure as an outline prepared in advance with appropriate Roman numerals and capital letters representing the major ideas arranged in some logical fashion. Once a first draft was completed, the focus was often on the correction of mechanical and grammatical errors.

During the 1970s, *writing as process* pointed to a different view of writing, one that permitted a far longer period for incubation of ideas and thoughts, one that emphasized multiple versions, flexibility, audience, nonlinear thinking, and peer review. A basic tenet of this approach was the possibility that the best route to a good paper was not a straight line. In this approach, a writer was more like a gardener than a railroad engineer.

Combined with the word processor, writing as process offers the prospect of *idea processing*. The word processor provides greater fluidity and flexibility than other writing technologies. It supports greater wordplay and association. The writer can try out dozens, even hundreds of variations until the resulting product is just right. The word processor actually makes thinking more powerful, *as long as students are taught how to use it in that way.*

Unfortunately, the word processor works little magic by itself. If the mechanics-driven approach to writing still dominates a school and department, the word processor will do little more than improve the appearance and mechanics of student writing (McKenzie, 1991).

In the adult world, many professional writers found that electronic text permitted rapid, risk-free early expression that could easily be cleaned up and modified later on. Writing, it soon became apparent, was not just what happened when you started moving a pen or began typing on a keyboard. Writing was also the development and refinement of ideas in one's mind. When someone ponders a writing challenge while showering, jogging, or driving, that reflection is part of the writing process. If the same person sits down, types a word on the monitor and asks for synonyms, that is writing. If the person starts stringing words together into sentences, either mentally, on paper, or on screen, all three are writing.

In writing as process, fragments are collected as beautiful beads that might later be strung in some ordered sequences. There is no early pressure for order and logic. The emphasis is on richness. The goal is to gather as many impressions, thoughts, and insights as possible without feeling constrained by critical and analytical judgments. Electronic text, because of its fluidity and malleability, is a wonderful medium for writers and thinkers.

What It Means to Communicate

Postman (1992) points out the lag between schools' emphasis on print media and the culture's preference for visual media. Few English departments offer an explicit curriculum to support the development of visual literacy. We also know that much communication between people, especially when they are face-to-face, is nonverbal. In a global village, the likelihood is strong that we will encounter important others—potential customers, clients, or competitors—from very different cultures, behaviors, and communication patterns. If we can learn to read the language of nonverbal communication across these cultures, we have a tremendous advantage.

Technologies are shifting our communication patterns rapidly and dramatically. Many people find, for example, that home voice mail means that we can nearly always leave a message for a friend, but we seem to have fewer actual conversations with these friends. Our airports are filled with travelers either taking down or leaving voice-mail messages. Many of these same people now find it hard to use the phone for human dialogue, the actual exchange of ideas. In contrast, users groups report that computer bulletin boards actually seem to encourage communication from those who might be shy at a face-to-face meeting. The technology often cuts several ways, and the way it cuts may result from default rather than conscious decision making.

Schools cannot afford to leave the development of student communication skills to chance.

Conclusion

New technologies promise to shift what we have long been calling "English" or "language arts" in the direction of "communication." Although the study of literature, grammar, and writing will remain extremely important, the way we read for information and compose our thoughts is undergoing a fundamental shift. By embracing the best of the new technologies and discarding the worst, teachers of English can equip their students with an invaluable skillset to accompany them into the next century.

High-Tech Arts

New technologies have been particularly slow to penetrate school arts programs, with the possible exception of the practical arts, where technology education has breathed new life into a curriculum that was previously fading in many districts.

Perhaps because artists have traditionally seen their role as protecting and giving expression to the human spirit, there has been a long history of artistic concern about the impact of technologies on the quality of human life, expressed through paintings, poetry, novels, dance, and drama. Even if the vast majority of the public embraces new technologies like television somewhat uncritically, the artistic community can be counted on to express skepticism.

When computers first arrived in schools, they offered more mathematical and scientific firepower than artistic potential. Early offerings of computer graphics and music were quite crude. Even as arts-related computer software began to grow in quality and power, there were still good reasons to challenge its value and to question its place in the arts curriculum.

Early computer art, especially that produced on the inexpensive, low-powered machines available in schools, often seemed counterfeit, a kind of glorified tracing machine allowing almost anybody to cut, paste, and modify someone else's clip art. Even those with no drawing ability of their own could suddenly produce printed results that appeared somewhat artistic. The printed results, emerging as they did from dot matrix printers, were far from impressive.

But was this computer output really art? There was tremendous doubt that this electronic cutting and pasting was art, even though some art teachers had been encouraging students to create collages from magazine clippings for decades (Hope, 1990).

Added to the skepticism that greeted the arrival of the new technologies was a long-standing tendency of schools to underfund arts programs during decades of concentration on so-called basics and a fiscal picture that often placed arts programs in jeopardy. Earnest art teachers have often been subjected to indignities such as "art on a cart" as school budgets have cut away the soul of programs and forced teachers to make do with inadequate supplies, limited schedules, and a lack of dedicated instructional space.

In accordance with a smokestack approach to education, the potential and importance of school arts programs has long been underestimated and underappreciated. Even though the kind of imaginative thinking engendered by the arts is winning attention and support in business circles, where innovation and creative problem solving are seen as key elements in global competition, the schools have been slow to develop that potential in students. In many communities, the arts are often considered "frills" and assigned a minor role.

Given this context, it is not surprising that technology rarely thrives in school art programs, and yet many enterprising teachers have pushed aside such obstacles to demonstrate that the new technologies can coexist with the traditional media in powerful ways, operating in tandem to extend their students' capabilities and sensibilities. This chapter argues the case that the arts deserve a place of prominence in a curriculum preparing students for the next century and that new technologies can enlist the enthusiastic participation of a far broader group of students than has been active in the arts in the past.

It is the arts that help us make sense of a troubling and often fragmented world, that help us to form wholes out of puzzle pieces and give our hearts solace through times of darkness. In part because the new technologies appearing throughout our world threaten to reduce the warmth, intimacy, and connectedness of our society, the arts offer a path to salvation. They keep us in touch with our deepest selves and help us to understand what needs understanding. They also set us free from old practices, old patterns, and old perspectives. They offer the joyful and playful chance to redesign and synthesize the elements of our world like great mosaics. They help us to challenge old paradigms and explore the negative space that is where our destiny probably lies.

Picture This, Imagine That

One reason to strengthen, deepen, and expand school art programs is the central role visual thinking will play in the society and economy of the next century. The visual arts program can develop four crucial skills:

Interpretation of visual material. As mentioned in earlier chapters, much of our information already travels in visual forms such as bar graphs and TV ads. Literacy in this decade and the next will extend beyond text and numeracy. We need citizens who can interpret the nuances of photographs, video, paintings, and graphical displays, exploring both the literal and the figurative dimensions.

By making choices about such aspects as composition, perspective, and light, the visual artist transforms images and changes their effect on the viewer. The artist may wish to provoke or evoke certain reactions or moods. In many cases, especially for those with little visual literacy, these effects may operate more or less subliminally, but an effective art program would equip students to think about and experience such material at a more conscious level. They should become aware of techniques as well as messages, asking how various effects were achieved.

New technologies may develop this awareness of technique by empowering students to step inside the visual invention process and by allowing them to tour the art collections of the world using videodiscs (B. Schwartz, 1991). Software programs such as Adobe *Photoshop* permit students to transform a photographic image, for example, into hundreds of different versions by manipulating a dozen diverse aspects such as contrast and color. The menus contained in such programs make the choices explicit for the student.

Smokestack art technologies also permitted much experimentation with visual media, but the choices were often less explicitly evident to students and the costs of experimentation were higher, in the sense that the time required to test out various choices was much higher than is the case with the new technologies. Changing the contrast in a photographic print, for example, required processing a piece of paper through a chemical bath. *Photoshop* requires nothing more than a click of the mouse. Programs such as DiVA *VideoShop* and *MacroMind Director* enable students to manipulate video segments in a similarly powerful manner.

Oftentimes, because the art program became mostly elective after middle school in smokestack systems, a limited and narrow segment of the student population was exposed to the kind of visual thinking that included exploration of various production techniques and their diverse effects. Power learning would involve all students in such experiences right on through high school.

Exploration of ideas and feelings. Visualization is often the parent of invention. The history of science and technology is full of anecdotes documenting discoveries evolving out of mental play with visual images, from Newton to Einstein. The base of the word *imagination* is, of course, *image*. The mind that can manipulate images fluidly and flexibly is well on the way to originality.

The art program could be the training ground for visual thinking of all kinds, and we could expect skills developed in that setting to transfer to other areas such as math and science where graphical representations of data, as shown in previous chapters, are becoming increasingly important. Once students learn to transform the physical aspects of an object by changing its elements, they can also begin to alter the figurative dimensions. This same kind of play moves readily into the realm of metaphor, where thinkers may employ various pictures in their "minds' eyes" to explore very complex scientific phenomena. Einstein first grasped the concept behind his theory of relativity, for example, by imagining several trains passing each other.

Synthesis, the skill of modifying the elements of some object or process in order to invent a better version, has received insufficient attention in schools, but the art program can afford students with many opportunities to play with such elements until they are pleased with their new version—kneading a lump of clay, for instance, until it becomes the upper torso of a discus thrower or disco dancer.

New technologies are not necessary for invention to occur in the art classroom, but they do have some spectacular advantages that make them excellent partners to tempera, paper, and clay. Whereas many of the traditional art materials and technologies place a premium on invention and thought *prior* to execution, the new technologies permit a very high level of experimentation and play *throughout* much of the production process. They make it very easy to backtrack, erase, and change course. By reducing the costs and consequences of "mistakes," new technologies support risk-taking and experimentation.

New technologies also support a more playful approach to production by automating some of the more tedious and time-consuming chores, such as filling in areas with various patterns and colors. The young artist can try out a dozen different colors and patterns in one section of a picture in less than 5 minutes, a feat that might take several days using the traditional art technologies.

Once an image or series of images has been created using a program such as Adobe *Illustrator* or Aldus *Freehand*, it remains much more fluid than it would with traditional art media and technologies, permitting many generations of student changes. A watercolor wash dries. It can be scratched, reawakened with fresh moisture, and modified by the application of new washes, but the options begin to narrow as the artist proceeds through the creative process. Watercolor also has a mind of its own, spreading across the paper in somewhat surprising ways. The artist can do little to reverse the process if it proves to be an unpleasant surprise. Computerized drawing and painting programs not only allow one to erase each move, they facilitate storage of various generations so the artist can return to an earlier version if desirable.

The fluidity of art software is made worthwhile by the array of tools available to manipulate the image. Adobe *Illustrator*, for example, enables the artist to magnify or minify the whole image or any part of the image in a matter of seconds. One can stretch, rotate, reverse, or duplicate any element. One can select from thousands of colors and apply them at great speed.

By making experimentation easier and less risky, the new technologies may broaden the group of students who experience success in the arts program and awaken a wider constituency to an appreciation for this form of thinking and communicating. As noted earlier, the free exploration of ideas and feelings closely parallels the kind of visual play that is powerfully supported by these new technologies. Because there may be very strong emotional and psychological components to such artistic exploration and expression, there is the promise of raising a generation more in tune with those dimensions of life whenever they are asked to think about any issue or challenge.

Development of insight. The kinds of thinking associated with the visual arts will help students "get the big picture." Just as systems theory prepares us to see both the forest and the trees, the visual arts help us to integrate the many complex pieces of life's puzzle until they form some kind of integrated whole. Because the human journey has always proven frustrating and perplexing, the arts have tried to provide illumination, reading patterns in the blowing sands or in the flight of starlings. Management consultants such as Senge (1990) claim that the success of organizations in the next few decades will depend on their ability to form learning teams with shared visions constructed from individual visions based on what he calls "personal mastery." With the help of the arts, according to Senge, we can learn to integrate reason and intuition, note our connectedness with the world, develop compassion, and establish commitment to the whole.

Communication of ideas and feelings. Without the power to share one's insights clearly and persuasively, profound understandings may remain locked inside where they will do little good for the society. If "a picture is worth a thousand words" and visual communication will be basic to the Information Age, then the visual arts program certainly becomes basic to the school experience—for all students. Given the fact that the adult society relies on a mixture both of traditional art forms and the new electronic media, it makes sense that an arts program should involve students in both as well.

As many schools move toward what is often called "authentic assessment," students are expected to conclude major units of study with some kind of "performance" that demonstrates that they have achieved significant insights during the learning process. The arts in combination with the new technologies will prove to be great allies in this undertaking. We would expect to see students developing visual essays combining text and pictures, some of which may be original art and some of which may be the results of cut-paste-and-modify techniques. We would expect to see students generating documentaries on local and state issues employing all manner of new technologies such as desktop video.

When students become the producers of knowledge rather than mere consumers, they may also develop both greater need for the arts and a greater appreciation for the arts. New technologies, because they provide a much broader group of students with artistic understandings and capabilities, serve to democratize what has too long been a narrow and overly specialized slice of the overall school program.

Variations on a Theme

Given a set of speakers, an electronic keyboard, an amplifier, MIDI software, and a computer, students can explore and compose music with much of the flexibility and imagination shown in the visual arts (Moore, 1992). Software programs project visual images of Beethoven's *9th Symphony* across the computer screen as it is being played on the speakers so that students may see the intertwining voices. They may then manipulate the elements of that music in ways analogous to many of the functions available with graphics programs, changing the tempo, the key, the rhythm, and the actual notes of various sections. They may also play elements of the music in isolation or various combinations in order to analyze their contribution to the whole.

If students wish to compose their own music, they can sit and toy with notes on the electronic keyboard, asking the computer to remember what they have played. Later they can play back their improvisations in order to identify sections worth saving. Cutting and pasting, they can begin putting together a collection of notes much like the necklace of words described in Chapter 5. All of this can be saved for future play and modification, and more complex orchestration can be added to what began as a simple tune or melody.

As in the visual arts, the new technologies make musical composition and creation accessible to a broader group of students. Once again we see a shift from consumption to production. The arts are no longer the bastion of a tiny minority.

The Play's the Thing

Multimedia brings so much visual and artistic material to the click of a mouse that it becomes increasingly easy for students to compare and contrast the interpretations of four different actors or dancers, for instance. Four different video segments can share the screen simultaneously in four different windows as the viewer plays and replays segments of a pas de deux or Macbeth's final speech.

Whereas citizens of the past century were lucky to ever see a live performance of Shakespeare, students in this decade can enjoy far more live performances, a great variety of broadcast performances, and a tremendous assortment of performances stored on electronic media that will increasingly become available over an electronic highway linking all schools and classrooms. As with electronic text, artistic performances, once digitized, will become far more easily retrievable in bits and pieces sorted and sifted by infotectives wishing to experience what art can show us about various human issues. A word search for both *sound* and *fury* contained in the same paragraph or measure might quickly turn up 60 poems, dramatic scenes, paintings, and dances, all of which cast light on (illuminate) those concepts.

The richness of the resources delivered by these technologies frees the student from the tyranny of individual artists' interpretations and gives license to the student's own imaginative recasting or replaying of various segments. The student once more can grow past the consumption of others' art to the production of his or her own art. When it is their turn to play Lady Macbeth or dance *Swan Lake*, they can manage personal variations on the themes they have witnessed and explored with the assistance of multimedia machines of various kinds. Videotaping their own rehearsals, they can insert theirs on-screen alongside the others they have viewed and keep adjusting their interpretation until they are content.

A Note of Caution

The minefield between the fine arts and pop culture deserves our thoughtful attention. We must take care not to stress production at the cost of quality. Craft must be guided by aesthetics, an appreciation of what constitutes beauty. Just because new technologies make artistic production quick and easy does not mean that the results are actually fine art. At the same time, pop culture is worthy of consideration and inclusion in our school programs, as a hot dog with hot mustard may violate nutritional good sense but make a Coney Island visit supremely enjoyable. If students have opportunities to move back and forth with guidance between the fine arts and pop culture, employing both the traditional and the new media, they will be able to avoid the "cookie cutter" nonsense that can easily emerge from either a computer or a pair of scissors.

Conclusion

Artists of all kinds have long found irony a welcome playmate and companion in the search for insight. It is especially intriguing, therefore, to note that the arts programs in many schools have been among the last to recognize the potential of new technologies to elevate their course of study to a position of prominence.

Although it is true that someone must hold the line against uncritical acceptance of new technologies and although it is true that much that attempts to pass as art or music in this electronic age is more "plastic" than aesthetically pleasing, schools owe their students a solid experience in both the traditional art forms and the new media as the arts remain one of the most crucial civilizing agents in a society that suffers from swirling currents of change threatening to isolate us and undermine both compassion and sensibility.

Annotated Bibliography

American Association for the Advancement of Science (AAAS). (1989). *Science for all Americans: Summary, Project 2061.* Washington, DC: Author.

Outlines a comprehensive approach to redesigning science instruction to prepare students for the next century.

American Society for Training and Development (ASTD) and the U.S. Department of Labor. (1988). *Workplace basics: The skills employers want.* Alexandria, VA: Author.

Provides an overview of the kinds of skills that are required by the Information Age workplace.

Applebee, A. (1986). *The writing report card: Writing achievement in American schools.* Princeton, NJ: Educational Testing Service.

Reports the writing achievement of students on the NAEP.

Ballard, R. (1992, October). *The Jason project—Sharing undersea adventure through technology.* Speech presented at the annual technology and learning conference of ITTE, Dallas, TX.

Describes program permitting students to join "live" underwater oceanographic expedition through satellite TV links.

Barker, J. (1992). *Future edge: Discovering the new paradigms of success.* New York: William Morrow.

Provides an overview of how paradigms can block change. Offers strategies for organizational success in making the paradigm shifts required by new conditions.

Catford, L., & Ray, M. (1991). *The path of the everyday hero.* Los Angeles: Jeremy P. Tarcher.

Defines the everyday hero and shows how heroes optimize their creative potential using four basic traits: observation, questioning, faith in creativity, and open-mindedness.

Crawford, L., & Molder, S. (1992). *Innovation in an integrated middle school curriculum: Systems thinking, a way of looking at our world.* Princeton, NJ: Educational Testing Service.

Reports the results of a middle school project employing systems thinking in conjunction with computer models.

Frye, S. (1989). The NCTM standards—Challenges for all classrooms. *Arithmetic Teacher, 9,* 4-7.

Outlines the implications of the NCTM standards for classroom mathematics teachers.

Ga Coté, R., & Diehl, S. (1992, June). Searching for common threads. *Byte,* pp. 290-305.

Explores the future of text searching software programs and how they will shift the way we store and process information.

Henkoff, R. (1992, October 19). Where will the jobs come from? *Fortune.*

Projects employment trends into the next decade.

Hope, S. (1990). Technique and arts education. *Design for Arts in Education, 6,* 2-14.

Explores the benefits and pitfalls of new technologies in the arts education field.

IBM (1992). *Science Success Stories.*

Describes school programs that have made effective use of IBM's science-related technologies.

Jones, L. (1992). *The 1990 science report card. NAEP'S assessment of fourth, eighth, and twelfth graders.* Princeton, NJ: Educational Testing Service.

Reports student difficulty with tasks requiring higher order thinking and a lack of enthusiasm for science as a career.

Mandinach, E., & Cline, H. (1992a). *The impact of technological curriculum innovation on teaching and learning activities.* Paper presented at AERA.

Describes the reaction of various types of teachers to the kinds of changes required by the introduction of systems thinking and computer modeling programs. Outlines strategies to enhance success.

Mandinach, E., & Cline, H. (1992b). *The implementation of technology-based curriculum innovations in classroom settings: Perspectives on methods and designs.* Princeton, NJ: Educational Testing Service.

Explores research design issues resulting from the organizational change associated with the introduction of new technologies to school settings.

Martin, W. (1980). Citizenship results from National Assessment. *Educational Leadership, 1,* 39-40.

Reports disappointing results on the NAEP social studies assessment.

McKenzie, J. (1991, June). Measuring results: What happens to student writing with the word processor? *From Now On,* pp. 3-7.

Demonstrates that word processing can significantly alter the way students reason and express themselves, but only if teachers come to understand how the new technology promotes flexibility and attention to more than mechanics.

Moore, B. (1992). Music, technology, and an evolving curriculum. *NASSP Bulletin, 544,* 42-46.

Outlines the potential of new technologies to support school music programs.

Morrissett, I. (1981). *Social studies in the 1980s. A report of Project SPAN.* Alexandria, VA: ASCD.

Describes the predominant practices characteristic of American social studies classrooms.

Naisbitt, J. (1982). *Megatrends: Ten new directions transforming our lives.* New York: Warner Books.

Identifies major trends influencing social change during the past decade.

National Alliance of Business (NAB). (1987). *The fourth r: Workforce readiness.* Washington, DC: Author.
Clarifies the kinds of employees business will need during the next few decades and explains what schools might do to meet those needs.

National Council for the Social Studies (NCSS). (1989). *Charting a course: Social studies for the 21st century.* Washington, DC: Author.
Provides a curriculum to prepare students for the next century.

Postman, N. (1992). *Technopoly.* New York: Alfred A. Knopf.
Criticizes the unthinking and uncritical manner in which society and schools have embraced new technologies. Calls the influx "cultural AIDS."

Schwartz, B. (1991). The power and potential of laser videodisc technology for art education in the 90's. *Art Education, 3,* 8-17.
Discusses the advantages of videodiscs in supporting arts programs.

Schwartz, P. (1991). *The art of the long view.* New York: Doubleday/Currency.
Explains the techniques involved in scenario building.

Senge, P. (1990). *The fifth discipline: The art and practice of the learning organization.* New York: Doubleday/Currency.
Outlines strategies to build organizations committed to constant growth, improvement, and change, relying on systems thinking and organizational development.

Toffler, A. (1990). *Power shift.* New York: Bantam.
Explains how influence is shifting to those nations and organizations with the most talent at utilizing information.

White, M. (1984). The electronic learning revolution: Questions we should be asking. *Prospects: Quarterly Review of Education, 1,* 23-33.
Promotes the importance of critiquing new technologies and teaching students visual literacy.

Zuboff, S. (1988). *In the age of the smart machine.* New York: Basic Books.

Reports on the introduction of information technologies in various industries, explaining benefits and problems associated with such change. Coins the term "infomating" to refer to information systems elevating human skills.